Ellie Charlton Age 6

Other titles in this series:
TO MOM (USA) TO MUM (UK, Australia)
TO DAD (you poor old wreck)
HAPPY BIRTHDAY! (you poor old wreck)

Third edition published simultaneously in 1997
by Exley Publications in Great Britain and
Exley Giftbooks in the USA.
Second edition published in Great Britain in 1990
by Exley Publications.
First edition published in Great Britain by Exley
Publications in 1975, revised and updated in 1990.

Exley Giftbooks
232 Madison Avenue, Suite 1206,
New York, NY 10016, USA.

Exley Publications Ltd,
16 Chalk Hill, Watford, Herts WD1 4BN,
United Kingdom.

Copyright © Richard and Helen Exley, 1975
Copyright © Richard and Helen Exley, 1990, 1997
ISBN 1-85015-846-0

A copy of the CIP data is available from the
British Library on request.

PRINTING HISTORY
First edition 1975
Nineteenth printing 1990

Second edition 1990
Eighth printing 1994

Designed by Richard Exley.
Front cover drawing by Alison
Fogg, age 8.
Back cover drawing by Cindy,
age 8.

Typeset by Delta, Watford, Herts.
Printed and bound in the UAE.

Grandmas & Grandpas
(you lovable old things)

EXLEY

NEW YORK • WATFORD, UK

The original version of GRANDMAS AND GRANDPAS was the book that launched our publishing company. We had little idea when it first appeared in the 1970s that it would prove so abidingly popular, reprinting year after year as successive generations of families recognized the funny, candid, loving and sometimes cryptic portrayal of grandparents by their grandchildren.

Now we have revised the book and included new pictures and words. All the entries and pictures in the book are by children. Nothing has been changed – not even the sometimes amazing grammar and spelling. A few were badly written, or went on about grouchy grandmas. But the overwhelming majority of entries tell a kind of love story; each one presents a personal little cameo, each one tells of a grandparent who is precious to a child. Sometimes the child doesn't seem to be aware of much more than the chocolates and the gifts. Many of the entries from the younger children make grandma sound like a walking ice-cream factory. But very soon, especially among the girls, something else emerges. They begin to appreciate the time a grandparent has to give. Many letters talked of gran or grandpa as a "best friend".

We've had great fun editing this new edition and we hope it brings families everywhere great joy. The book is a kind of "Thank you" for all the bandaged knees, apple pies and bedtime stories – and the lessons in life so freely given. One summed up the feeling very simply: "We try to pay her back for her kindness to us. But it would take for ever."

Enjoy the book. The children say it all, with such perception.

Richard & Helen Exley

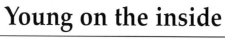

A grandma is old on the outside and young on the inside.

John Wright *Age 7*

The age of my Grandma
is young.
She can do
all the things
around the house.
She takes me
to the park.
My Grandma
likes playing football
and rollercoaster
and loves running.

Mandy Tiwana *Age 11*

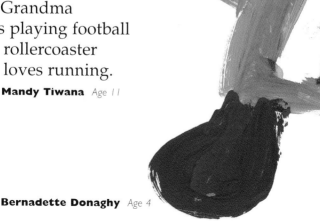

Bernadette Donaghy *Age 4*

Definitions

A grandfather is the one who helps you with your homework, even when he doesn't know how to do it.

Gary

A Grandmother is a lady who either sleeps or knits.

Sara Spurrier *Age 12*

Grandmothers are...

Generous giving people
Regular churchgoers
Afternoon snoozers
Never (well, hardly ever) irritated by you
Drinkers of whisky and water
Members of a ladies' church group
Owners of old jalopies
Crossword fanatics
Hospitable hostesses
Eaters of brocolli, spinach, cabbage and beans
Relaters of gossip
Scrabble players
    and without Grandmothers,
the world would be a different place.

H. Bulley

Grandmothers are people who still do the spring cleaning.

Maureen Dracey

She's the person who tells me all the things about my parents, they would rather not have me know.

Sarah Scott *Age 15*

Carl Price *Age 6*

My Grandpa is tough outside, but soft hearted inside.

Justin Birch *Age 10*

Grandparents are cheerful, sentimental old things.

Donna Pearce *Age 12*

Grandpas

A Grandad is a person you never forget, never. I'm proud that he's my grandad.
And I'll never forget his hand in mine as we walk down the street together.

Suzanne Cairns *Age 13*

I think my grandpa is fantastic, most grandpas are. If you are saving up for something they are like walking piggy banks and give you money.

Jeremy Shilling

My grandfather is not really like any old man, for he is 86 years old and has a special driving license and swims in ice cold lakes in which I would never dare to put my foot. A person must not think of him as a first class madman, or at least a person can think as a person wants but I still think and will think he is the nicest and most considerate person I have had to bump into.

P. Ham *Age 13*

My Grandmother is crumpled.

Richard Humphrey

Some grandmothers are very small and some grandmothers are bery big. You can get all different sized grandmothers, you know.

Andrew Deboata *Age 8*

The thing that makes grandmas so jolly looking is the fact that as they get older they grow out instead of up.

Jacqueline Hope

Mine looks funny. She has got a long face and her chin wobbels when she walks.

Michael Barbridge *Age 7*

My grandparents aren't all crooked and bent. But I doubt if they're old enough yet.

Philip Paddon *Age 12*

Caroline Pentland *Age 5*

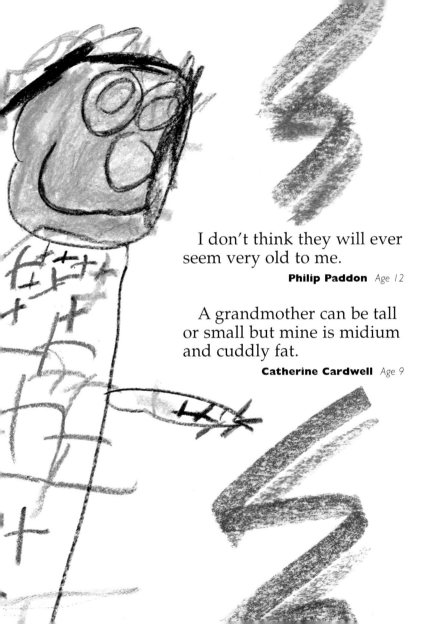

I don't think they will ever seem very old to me.

Philip Paddon *Age 12*

A grandmother can be tall or small but mine is midium and cuddly fat.

Catherine Cardwell *Age 9*

Sandra Rendall Age 10

My Grandparnts are very nice to me.
When we leave they cry.

Vanessa Coppeck *Age 9*

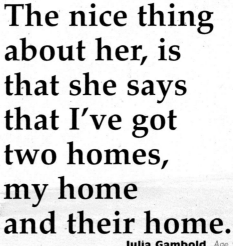

The nice thing about her, is that she says that I've got two homes, my home and their home.

Julia Gambold *Age 9*

Old wrecks

Grannies used to be old with grey hair. But nowadays grannies can be quite young.

Amanda Weisberg *Age 7*

Grandmas say that the title makes them feel old – like a Grand piano, I suppose.

Isobel Blaber *Age 14*

Grandpa is over 40 and under 90.

Alexander Hambly *Age 10*

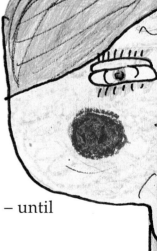

They aren't young, But my dad's catching up.

N. Arthur

When they tell my parents Not to be childish I feel very, very young.

Peter Wilson

I Thought Dad was rather old – until I met grandpa.

Ian Laing *Age 13*

I wonder does she feel young inside....

Catherine Lawlor *Age 11*

My Grandparent's are both conciderate. They are both about the same age but that doesn't seem to bother them.

Elizabeth Rose

My grandmother is getting older than she thinks.

Clive Owen *Age 10*

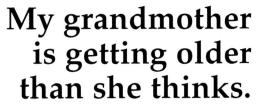

Grandmothers'
bones
are old.

Amanda Weisberg *Age 7*

Caroline Curtis *Age 11*

Grandparents live in their own
funny world where time seems To
go backwards. **Kevin J. Brown** *Age 12*

Yesterday

She's called "Nana" and she tells tales
that she told to mother when she
was a child. Many stories of exciting
adventures that happened a long
time ago. They did not have the
luxuries that we have, but
waltzing in their large living
room when the furniture was
pushed aside, singing round
the piano, telling stories by
the blazing fire whilst they
ate hot muffins. Skating on
the frozen lake in winter,
riding in a steam train, all
these more than make up for
television and trips abroad. I
hope my Nana will stay with
me for a long time, and when
I have the farm I long for, she
will be able to live with me
and feed the chickens. We
will have a blazing log fire
and she will tell us stories of
the past. **Dawn Williams** *Age 10*

David Byrne

A refuge

She now is a grandmother, a person who shares
A person who loves and a person who cares,
Her face has an expression of understanding and
  love,
Of normal standards she towers above.
Her time to all is so generously given,
              A person who I'm sure is destined
                  for heaven.

Sally Lloyd Jones *Age 14*

A Refuge

When you go to her with your pride bruised and
hurt; she never takes sides, but helps you to think
fairly and to see the other person's point of view.
She knows the problems that all the members of
her family go through, and is able, from her own
  experience to give advice. She is usually a
  sympathetic listener – to what must seem to her,
    your personal inconsequential (compared with
      some of the ones that she has to face during
        her life-time) problems. She never tries to
advise her children on grand-children, unless she
is asked to do so, and lives her own life, so as not
to be a nuisance, but close enough to be a help in
a crisis. In short a grandmother is a refuge.

Amanda Evans

Bribery

It's very noisy in our house and when Grandma comes over she says, If you can be quiet I'll give you some spending money. And we are quiet then for a little while.

Joe Cassidy *Age 12*

Grandmas are very necessary for letting you do things you are not allowed to do generally, like watching "The Late Night Horror Movie" or eating too many waffles than are good for you, or not making you eat carrots.

Kate Clancy *Age 14*

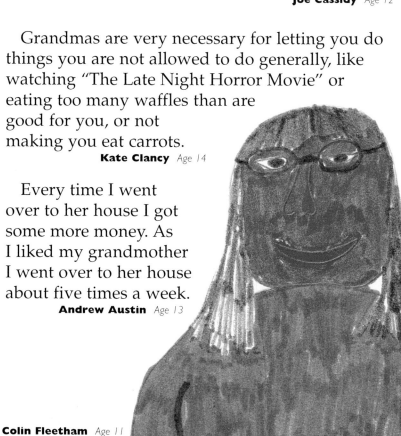

Every time I went over to her house I got some more money. As I liked my grandmother I went over to her house about five times a week.

Andrew Austin *Age 13*

Colin Fleetham *Age 11*

One of a grandmother's most prized privileges is to spoil her grandchildren. She arrives armed with pockets full of goodies, and special pocket-money to buy the child the things denied it by its parents for numerous good reasons – no cheesecakes because they have too much sugar for example. Granny stuffs the child full of ice cream and cakes, and then leaves before it is sick.

Tessa Ing

The 'grandmother' is usually a great source of the children's income as she nearly always gives them quite a lot of money after a happy but exhausting visit. The money is usually for all her grandchildren ("little angels"). They usually stick their hands out suggestively or start whining that they can't afford a teddy bear or a skiing trip.

Charles Robert Fenwick Linfoot *Age 13*

It's a pity about their teeth!

My Grandma has special toothpaste and pretending teeth.

Clive Smith *Age 7*

Once she lost her teeth later
when I was running the bath
they floated to the top.
I think she is very typical.

S. Enright

They often have a few
false teeth Which in the
morning are often found out
Which lie besides the bed
which are quite frightening
They look like elephants fangs.

Helen Turner

If theres one thing that
annoys me about her is, she
clicks her false teeth and she
does it when theres any music
going keeping in time with
the tune.

Alison Brice

My Grand Mother is very unusual.
She has a very funny face.
Shes got silver hair and only four teeth left.
I fink she should have two teeth out that
will leave two.

David Fitzgibbon *Age 7*

"Will you look at that" shouted Grandpa and took out his false teeth and shook them at the driver who had just passed us. (Grandpa does not like being passed he hardly ever is though because he drives at such a speed). When we came up behind him, Grandpa waved his false teeth and shouted "You crazy old fool".

D. Farnworth

Andrew Clissold *Age 12*

My special Grandmother

Her mask was of wrinkled skin
Attached onto her face.
It was not really her because it did not fit
It belonged to another time and place.
But the more she talked and as I watched her
She shed the mask from her face.

A light as new as spring shone in her eyes
And in her movements a youthful grace.

Age is but a word of time
A thing which we created.
A thing which is measured like the bleeps on a
　radio.
But who can measure grandmothers
And put them into hours and minutes
Of knowledge kindness love and care?

My Grandmother is no diagem or paste
But a clear and sparkling diamond.

Jacqueline Solomons *Age 9*

Now she needs me

When I was young and cut my knee
She would become an enfolding,
   purple curve of sympathy.

If I was caught doing, any wrong thing
   She would be a rectangle, dark blue
   glowing.

If in dire need of help am I
She is a pulsating orange pillar,
That touches the sky.

When something special I have
Into a bouncing restless globe,
   she will go
Of a beautiful sunflower yellow.

To the dismal depths of depression
   I have been
So she has become a pyramid
   of gentle green.

When she is ill
And I make her jovial
A blazing turquoise star,
tells me I'm her cheering up pill.

Funny, and strange, how time
  should change.
Amazing how time should beg
I needed her once now she needs
  me.

Quentin Radford *Age 11*

Carrie Campion *Age 5*

Grandmothers used to be formal, strict, old fashioned and covered in slippery black dresses tinkling with jet trinkets and smell of mothballs. My father's mother is a grandmother but she is comfortable and warm and soft, scented with cologne and baking.

E. J. Slessenger

Sandra Dale Age 9

As you have proberly noticed my granny thinks time stands still and wears the same clothes as when she was small (except a few sizes bigger).

Paul Milsom *Age 10*

A Grandmother tells you to put on a coat or you will catch a cold.
A Grandmother fusses over you.
A Grandmother wears old fashioned clothes.

Angela Mutch *Age 11*

Grandmothers wear quite long coats to cover up their knobbly knees.

Carol Stacey *Age 7*

Old in the world of the young

A Grandmother is an elderly person who watches people walk past and hopes that someone will come and visit them.

Simon Martindale *Age 10*

Grandmothers are the old in the world of the young, and are continually having the "good old days" wiped out of the conversation.

Rita Bourke

They long to help and yearn to be loved.

Rita

A Grandmother is a little old lady, who comments on the weather and how tall you are getting, tells everyone the latest gossip and all about her son who came to see her.

Jackie Thompson

Grandmothers always come up with advice, which is given whether you need it or not.

Rita

When she is sitting by herself she looks old and loney. But when she has company she looks young again.

Mary O'Gorman *Age 11*

Julia

Lovey, dovey...

My grandmommy loves my granddad and my granddad loves my grandmommy. Sometimes they get mad at each other and they fight. I feel bad. When they get lovey dovey again and kiss I feel good.

Kimberley *Age 5*

The only time my grandma is sad is when she washes Grandads socks.

Natalie Hall *Age 9*

A grandad is a earbox for a grandmother to say things to.

Nicola Hankinson *Age 11*

my grandpa and grandma love each other because they hold hands and he keeps telling her silver threads among the gold.

Sarah Anderson, Age 8

Sarah Barnes *Age 9*

Toughies

Some peoples grandmas are tough old ladies, if you say they are too old to do something, they will say "Don't be silly, I could walk a mile in a minute.

Belinda Spark *Age 11*

Some grandmas are the kind that look frail on the outside, but on the inside they are the dangerous kind, that bash policemen and robbers on the head with umbrellas and handbags if they get angry.

Belinda Spark *Age 11*

My Grandma is very game for her age. I distinctly remember, one day, when she took me on an outing to a park, and she said to me, shall we run round the Fish Pond, shouting at the top of our voices? and when I asked her why, she said she felt like doing something naughty.

Jane Townson *Age 10*

Some odd habits

Grandmothers are fat and put wigs on before they go to the door.

Richard Dunmow *Age 8*

My Grandma has a good habbit of eating cake every evening. I like this because I have some too.

Nicholas Dunne *Age 11*

My Gram has a habbit of naming things she calles her freezer Fredda and her two radios big willy and little willy.

Allison Anthony *Age 10*

Perhaps the best definition of the grandmother, is somebody who spent her time telling your mother what not to do, when she was young. And now spends her time, criticism your mother for giving you the same advice.

Calvin Giles *Age 12*

My Great Grandad has a habit of buying me chocolates and then eating them.

Jay Coquillon

Jacqueline Hollely *Age 10*

A faint aroma
of gingerbread
and all good
things mixed
together,
seems to
linger
all around
a grandmother.

Elspeth Gordon *Age 12*

Rachael Bolton *Age 7*

A Granny is jolly and when she laughs a warmness spreads over you.

J. Hawksley *Age 11*

A Grandmother is kind and doesn't like all the new coins and other small change – she gives us them quite happily.

Bobby Marston

A Grandmother doesn't criticize.

Anne Joplin *Age 11*

Donna Longville

Lovely people

My christening gown was made from her wedding dress. History for me is memories for them, yet they are not aged or dusty: Grandma and Grandpa are real. A whole part of my childhood would be missing if I had not known them. With them I am at once a little girl and an object of pride and hope for the future.

E. J. Slessenger

Every time children go there most of them say "come in deary hallo pet" and all lovely words like that.

Sarah Keen *Age 8*

Grandmothers and Grandfathers give a home a friendly touch.

Marco Orlandini *Age 9*

Grandpas

Grandad is mad about Football he was a player once but now he is to old so when he trys to kick a ball sometimes he falls over.

Kaal Page *Age 9*

My Grandad pretends he has a jelly bean tree.

William Sholl *Age 8*

Grandpas always have a bag of tasty goodies in their pockets well as lots of junk and odds and ends, such as a penknife, string, a compass, an animal bone and a toy soldier.

Fiona Gibbings

Grandfathers like cabbage and caulieflower and other awful things.

Beth *Age 10*

My grandad teases me a lot but realy he is not a teaser but just a kind old man.

Mark Moulding *Age 8*

My Grandpa used to rough and tumble with my brother. But now both of them are past it.

Richard Thompson *Age 12*

A grandfather is somebody who outbalds Kojak.

Nicholas

Anthony Day Age 10

Memories

She sits there living,
In her memories,
The young men, the laughter
The river boats, Summer picnics and romance,
Romance unlike any other,
Special, strong and Everlasting.

Nothing is left now,
Only memories,
Though life goes on, but
She cannot understand
Remembering her long quiet childhood,
Which no longer remains,
Life was simple,
And days were long and happy
Children now are so restless
And unloving, taking everything
For granted, awaiting their maturity
Wasting their long, lazy days
Of innocence
Oh, how can she make them understand?

Susan Legg *Age 15*

Emma Barlow

Spoils you rotten!!

Grandma's and Grandad's hardly ever tell you off so you have to look at your feet, with your head hung down and hands clenched together. They let you off as light as a feather.

Jennifer Norman *Age 12*

She lets you do what you shouldn't and if mom complains she says "Remember when you were little and I caught you dipping your finger in the sugar bowl? You're not too old to get your ears boxed".

Jackie Thompson

When my mother tells me to do something I do not want to do I tell my Grandmother and she talks my old lady out of it.

Sonia Allan *Age 10*

My granny lets me lick the cake mixture when she is finished. She lets me leave my food, and she spoils me so much that when I grow up I won't want anything.

Sandra Webb *Age 10*

My Grandmother is very patient. She would have to be with me around!

Helena Leeson *Age 10*

Your Granny loves you. No matter what you do.

Paul Myers *Age 10*

A grandpa is the person who helps you eat your food when you can't eat it all, so it looks like you at it all.

Farrah *Age 10*

Jenna Green *Age 6*

Reginald!

The best thing that I like about my Grandmother is, when she gets up in the morning and the heater's on she'll come and get dressed there. She'll stand by the heater and warm her behind and then my grandpa will come along and he stands there looking at me and then he looks at Grandma and he then gives a funny laugh, then creeps up to her and he rubs her fat tummy "Reginald" she shouts. Her face then glows and wrinkles up and her eyes are full of laughter, her cheeks are a pair of roses and her glasses fall on to her nose.

"Reginald", she shouts, "if you don't stop that I'll have a burn't behind."

Beverly Ward

Gemma Busby Age 6

Softies!

I love the magic
Grandad does,
especially the
peppermints
he makes appear
from my ear!

Rebecca Smith *Age 11*

Grandpa grows
great raspberries and
always pretends
not to notice
us eating them.

Tracey Knight *Age 8*

Samantha Weinstein *Age 9*

If you want
something
always give
your grandad
a hug.

Claire Elaine Picken
Age 9

Militant grannies

They appear on the strikers camp, with rolling pins
All armed to the teeth,
All ready to do battle with gnashing teeth,
One granny lets go with her Fiery left hook,
Which lands a union leader in the pond,
Where he floats on his back, like a dead duck,
They swing out left and right With all their might,
And strike down every enemy in their sight,
And as the strikers Flee the scene.
Then the grannies take up the chase,
They swing their handbags like a mace
They smash them down, one by one,
And as each one Falls,
All the grannies let out their victory calls.

Adrian John Bradley *Age 12*

Jenna Green *Age 6*

Inflation
Inflation they say
not like the
good old days.

Catherine Ashley *Age 9*

Andrew Barnett *Age 10*

Grumps and grumblers

Perhaps her most peculiar obsession was the sending back of letters. Whenever I wrote to her I would receive my letter back with red lines underneath each word I had spelt wrong. So I had to rewrite the letter correctly and if I spelt anything wrong again back the letter would come, with the same red lines again. Obviously one would write to her as little as possible.

Amanda Bond

Some days when we've been there too long they should be called a new names Grumppa and Groanie.

Alberto Fernandez *Age 8*

My Fathers Mother is rather grumpy she likes to watch the news and moans to us when she hears about bombs as if we had planted them.

Allison Anthony *Age 10*

All the time in the world

She has a past of her own and a future which belongs to everyone. She leads an empty life of her own which is filled by the lives of others. Most of all she is a person who will always have time to see you when the rest of the world is busy.

Gill Webb

Grandmas have todo

Katy *Age 8*

Grandmas are always slow but they do not mind for they have all the time in the world.

Malcolm Andrew Age 10

I love you because you are always happy for me to show you things other people don't bother to look at.

Katy Turner Age 8

and Grandpas

nothing

But talk

toyou

Love

My Grandmother is not plump but nice and comfortable, when she sits you on her knee you can nestle down and feel safe and secure.

Angela Dobson *Age 10*

We call her Nanny. She is not very old I don't mind how old she is. I would not want another nanny because ours is the nicest one. I wouldn't swop her for any sum of money.

Jane Clarke *Age 10*

If I have a secret I will always tell Grandmother not anyone else.

Joanna Simmonds *Age 8*

My grandma is in heaven but she was always helping other people so I know she is a very special angel.

Sharon Watson *Age 9*

Ryan Lloyd *Age 6*

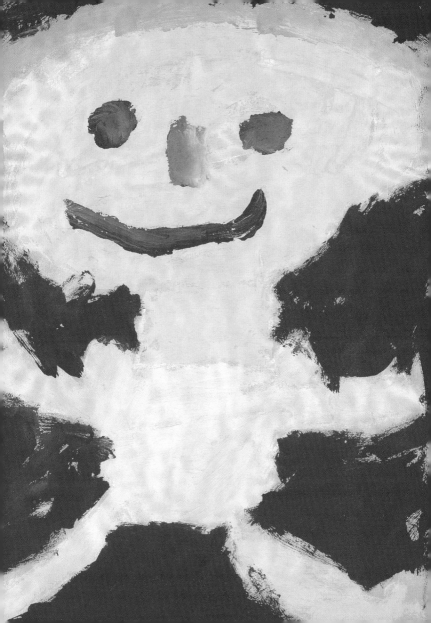